Turandot

G. RICORDI & C. S.p.A. - MILANO

TURANDOT

Lyric drama in three acts and five scenes

By GIUSEPPE ADAMI and RENATO SIMONI
Music by GIACOMO PUCCINI

The last duet and the finale of the opera were completed by
F. ALFANO

English version by R. H. ELKIN

RICORDI

Cover by Peter Hoffer

Printed in Italy - Imprimé en Italie

Reprint 1994

characters

PRINCESS TURANDOT	*Soprano*
THE EMPEROR ALTOUM	*Tenor*
TIMUR, The Dethroned Tartar King	*Bass*
THE UNKNOWN PRINCE Calaf, his son	*Tenor*
LIU, Young Slave Girl	*Soprano*
PING, The Grand Chancellor	*Baritone*
PANG, The General Purveyor	*Tenor*
PONG, The Chief Cook	*Tenor*
A MANDARIN	*Baritone*
THE PRINCE OF PERSIA	*Baritone*
THE EXECUTIONIER	*Baritone*

Imperial Guards — The Executioner's
Assistants — Children — Priests — Mandarins
Dignitaries — The Eight Wise Men
Turandot's Attendants — Soldiers
Standard Bearers — Musicians — Shades of
the Departed — The Crowd.

The action takes place in Peking, China, in legendary times.

Act first

The walls of the great Violet City; the City of the Celestial Empire. The stage is almost entirely enclosed by a semicircle of massive bastions. On the right, the curve is interrupted by a high covered portico sculptured all over with monsters, unicorns, phoenix, with pillars rising from the backs of huge tortoises.

At the foot of the portico, a heavy bronze gong is suspended from two arches.

On the bastions have been erected poles bearing te heads of the victims. On the left and in the background, three gigantic gates open from the walls. The curtain rises on a glorious sunset. In the distance, bathed in golden light, Peking is seen.

The square is thronged with a picturesque Chinese crowd motionless and listening to the words of a Mandarin. From the heights of the bastions, flanked by Tartar guards in black and red, he reads a tragic decree.

The Mandarin

People of Peking!
The law is this: — Turandot, the Chaste, shall be the bride of him of Royal lineage, who can solve her three enigmas. But he whose attempts are unsuccessful pays for his failure with his noble head!
The Prince of Persia has not been favoured by fortune: and, when the moon has risen, is doomed to die on the scaffold!

(The Mandarin withdraws and the crowd breaks up into increasing tumult)

The crowd

The scaffold! The scaffold! Hurry!
We must have the executioner!

Hurry! Hurry! He must die!
To the scaffold! He must die! Do not tarry!
If he's asleep, we'll drag him from his bed!
Pu-Tin-Pao! Pu-Tin-Pao! Pu-Tin-Pao!

(*The crowd tries to invade the bastions*)

        To the Palace! To the Palace!

The guards (*clashing with the crowd and trying to push them back*)

Get back, you rabble!

(*In the tumult, many are trampled under foot. There is a confused din of frightened people — shrieks — protests — pleadings*)

The crowd

Ah! Barbarians! Oh! my children! My poor old Mother!

The guards (*in pursuit*)

Get back, you rabble!

The crowd

        For the love of heaven! Pity!

Liù (*in despair*)

My poor master has fallen!

The guards

        Get back, you rabble!

Liù

Will not one of you come and help me to save his life?...
Oh! help!

(*She looks round imploringly. Suddenly a youth hastens to help her; he bends over the old man, then with a cry...*)

The unknown Prince

Father!... My father!... O father, have I found you!...
Look at me!.. Am I dreaming?...

(*He assists the prostrate man and kisses him, whilst Liù, drawing back, exclaims:*)

Liù

O my master!

The unknown Prince (*in great anguish*)

Father! Thy son is here! Listen! My father!
Forgotten all our pain... forgotten all our cruel woes, since
now the gods have granted our reunion!

Timur (*coming to, opens his eyes, gazes at his rescuer, hardly
believing it can be true, and cries:*)

Art alive, then? Thou! My son!

The unknown Prince (*terrified*)

Hush! Hush!

(*Aided by Liù, he succeeds in dragging Timur away from
the crowd. Then, in a broken voice, with tears, he says*):

The usurper of thy crown is seeking to track us!
And wherever we go, he will find us!

Timur

I have sought thee and thought, my son, thou must have
perished!

The unknown Prince

And I have mourned thee; Oh! let me kiss thy sainted
hands!...

Timur

My son, whom I was mourning!

The crowd (*which, meanwhile, has gathered together again
near the bastions, breaks into shouts of frantic joy:*)

The executioner's coming! Kill him! Kill him!

(*On the top of the walls, in lurid bloodstained rags, are
seen the executioner's assistants, grotesquely tragic, dragg-*

*ing the huge sword, which they proceed to sharpen on an
enormous whetstone. Timur, still prostrate on the ground,
in a subdued voice to his son, who bends over him:)*

Timur

...The battle lost and I, a poor old throneless King, was
fleeing, when I heard someone at my side who whispered
« Come with me and I will guide thee! »... It was Liù...

The unknown Prince

      ...Blessings upon thee!

Timur

And when I fell exausted, 'twas she who dried my bitter
tears and she who begged for me...

The unknown Prince (*gazing at the maiden, deeply moved*)

Liù, who art thou?

Liù

      I am nothing... just a slave, my lord...

The unknown Prince

But why didst thou share in all our suffering?

Liù (*with ecstatic joy*)

Just because, one day... in the Palace, thou didst smile
at me!

The crowd (*urging on the executioner's assistants*)

      Sharpen the whetstone! Grind it!

*(The two assistants who have wiped the blade, now hold
it to the whetstone and grind it furiously. The sparks fly;
they work with ferocity, singing a lurid song which is re-
echoed by the crowd)*

The executioner's assistants

Grind the sword until the blade is sharp and shining,
We are never slack or idle in the realm of Turandot!

The crwod

In the realm of Turandot!

The executioner's assistants

O hapless lovers, death awaits ye! with our instruments of torture.
We are all agog to see them rip your skin!
Fair and radiant as a jewel,
Cold as marble—cold and cruel,
Is the lovely Turandot!

The crowd

Lovers tender, come surrender!

The executioner's assistants

Strike the gong aloud and clear,
And the Princess will appear!

The crowd

Strike the gong aloud and clear,
And the Princess will appear!

The executioner's assistants (*with coarse laughter*)

When you've sounded the gong,
We will come along!
Love's unavailing, without a bit of luck!
Enigmas are there three and death is one!

The crowd

Enigmas are there three and death is one!

The executioner's assistants

Grind and sharpen! Till the shining blade with blood is dripping!
We are never slack or idle in the realm of Turandot!

The crowd

In the realm of Turandot!
(*Whilst the assistants depart to carry the sword to the*

executioner, the crowd forms itself into picturesque groups here and there, on the ramparts, watching the sky in wild expectation, as night discends slowly)

The crowd

Is the moon never coming? Shed thy light on us!
Rise in the heavens! Hasten! Quickly! Hasten!
O pallid visage! Hasten, thou lover of the departed!
Transparent! Silvery goddess! Diaphanous!
How impatiently the yawning graves are waiting thy
arising!

(One by one the pale rays of the moon shed their light)

Yonder a ray is dawning, to light the darkness with its silver radiance!

All *(with a shout of joy)*

Pu-Tin Pao! Pu-Tin-Pao! The moon has risen!

(The golden hue of the background has changed into a livid silvery colour — the cold whiteness of the moon is diffused over the ramparts and the city.

At the gate of the wall, guards dressed in long black tunics are seen.

A dismal dirge is heard. The procession is approaching, preceded by a group of children singing:)

The children

Over the hills far away
Doth the stork sing her lay,
But no spring has flowered yet
And the snow lies cold and wet.
Far across the desert can you hear
Thousand voices sighing clear:
Come o Princess, come down to me!
Then will melt the snow,
Summer here will be!

(The executioner's assistants advance, followed by the priests bearing funeral offerings. Then the Mandarin and the other dignitaries.

*After them walks, the young Prince of Persia, handsome
and almost childlike. At the sight of the victim, so timorous
and dreamy, with his white neck uncovered and a far-away
look in his eyes, the ferocity of the crowd is turned to pity.
As soon as the Prince of Persia has come on the scene, the
executioner appears; gigantic, tragic, carryng the huge
sword which rests on his shoulder)*

The crowd

Unhappy youth! Mercy! Mercy! Mercy!
— How courageous his bearing!
— Oh! how comely, what a fair and noble visage!
— In his eyes love is shining!
— Alas! Oh! pardon him! Alas! Have mercy!

The voice of the unknown Prince (*dominating the crowd*)

Ah, have mercy!

The crowd (*clamouring*)

Mighty Princess!

The unknown Prince

Come then, that I may see thee and curse thee! Thou
tyrant!

*(The words fade on his lips, for high in the imperial loggia,
Turandot appears. The moon, with her bright reflection, il-
luminates her; she seems almost ethereal, like a vision.
Her dominant power and proud bearing stem the tumult
as if by magic.
The crowd falls prostrate to the ground. Only the young
Prince of Persia, the executioner and unknown Prince re-
main standing).*

The unknown Prince (*in ecstasy*)

O divine apparition of beauty! O wonder!
Surpassing marvel!

*(He covers his face, dazzled. A short silence ensues. Tu-
randot makes an imperious gesture. It is the Death Sen-
tence. The executioner nods his head in assent. The mourn-*

ful irge is heard again, as the procession moves, ascends the walls and disappears beyond the bastions, the crowd following)

Priest robed in white in the procession

O great Koung-tsè!
May the spirits of the dying to thy presence rise!

(Their voices are lost — Turandot has departed and in the dim light of the Piazza, only Timur, Liù and the unknown Prince remain.
The Prince stands erect, as in ecstasy, under the influence of that vision of loveliness, which has fatally nailed him to his destiny.
Timur anxiously approaches and calls him to arouse him)

Timur

What art thou doing?

The unknown Prince

O wonder! My very soul is embalmed by her fragrance!

Timur

Thou'rt ruined!

The unknown Prince

O divine apparition! Wond'rous beauty!
Ah! me, my heart is stricken!

Timur

No! No! Hearken to me!
Liù! get him away! We must drag him from here!
Take his hand in thy own. We must not tarry!

Liù

O Sir! you're lost if you linger!

Timur

For life awaits us yonder!

The unknown Prince

My life is here, my father!

(*Freeing himself, he runs towards the gong which shines in a mysterious light and cries:*)

Turandot!...

(*But to his cry another cry responds*)

Turandot!...

(*It his the dying invocation of the young Prince of Persia, Then a muffled blow resounds.*

The cries of the crowd are now heard, violent and in quick succession, full of resentment

The unknown Prince hesitates one moment — then his obsession takes hold of him once more. The gong sparkles and flashes)

Timur

Are you to die like this?

The unknown Prince

Triumph and victory shall be mine and I shall win her!

(*He is about to throw himself against the gong, when suddenly between himself and the sparkling disc, three mysterious figures intervene. These are Ping, Pong and Pang, three grotesque masks, the Emperor's three Ministers: that is, the Grand Chancellor, the Chief Cook and the Purveyor General. The Unknown Prince starts back; Timur and Liù draw nearer to each other with frigth in the shadow.*

The gong is in darkness)

The Ministers (*turn upon the Prince and surround him*)

Come away at once, you idiot!
Who are you? What d'you want? Begone!
Madman, we warn you! Throught that gate lies every kind of butchery and torture!
Here they'll choke you — and bleed you!
— They will flay and slay you!

— And torture you and skin you!
— And slice you and skin you!
Don't lose another minute but return to your own country
and find a butcher there if you are longing for a shambles!
But not here! No, not here!

The unknown Prince (*violently*)

Stand back and let me pass!

The Ministers (*barring his way*)

The cemeteries here are overflowing!
— We've plenty of native madmen!
— We've no use for lunatics from elsewhere!
— Escape before a certain death awaits you!

The unknown Prince (*with increase violence*)

Stand back and let me pass!

The Ministers (*with comic compassion*)

— And all for a Princess!
    Pooh!.. What is she?
        Just a woman
            with a crown on her head
                and with a regal mantle!
                    But if you saw her naked,
                        — just flesh, like every other!
                            Not even flesh that's good for eating!

Ping

Oh! beware of women! Or else, espouse a hundred! For,
though you may not believe it, Turandot, that marvel, has
but one face and two arms and but two legs! Very fine,
I grant you — oh yes, very — but always the same ones!
But hundred wives, or even more,
And arms and legs you'll have galore!
Two hundred loving arms, a hundred pretty faces,
Hundreds of warm embraces!..

(*Bursting into loud laughter, he sidles up closer to the Prince*)

The unknown Prince (*violently*)

Stand back and let me pass!

(*A group of handmaidens lean over the balustrade of the Imperial loggia and with raised hands reprimand the disturbance*)

Turandot's serving maids

Be quiet there!
Who talks so loudly?
In slumber her eyes our Princess closes.
The gentle slumber of Turandot!
Not a sound may disturb this sacred hour!

The Ministers (*in protestation to the maids*)

Run away! you chatterboxes!

(*suddenly remembering that they had allowed the Prince his freedom for a moment*)

'Ware the gong! 'Ware the gong!

(*The maidens have withdrawn. The Prince, deep in thought, repeats:*)

The unknown Prince

Not a sound may disturb this sacred hour!

The Ministers (*pointing at him with their fingers and bursting into laughter*)

Look at him, Pang!
Look at him, Ping!
Look at him, Pong!
Hallucinated!
He is crazy!
He is loony!

Timur (*aside to Liù*)

He does not hear us, alas!

The Ministers (*with decision*)

Now! Let's try, all three!

(*They approach the Prince, then in a low voice, almost in
the rhythm of a fable recited by a child, they repeat
together:*)

Night without a ray or shimmer...

Chimney flue without a glimmer...

 Are more clear than the enigmas of Turandot!

Iron, flint or alabaster...

Or your stubborn pate, young master...

 Are less hard than the enigmas of Turandot!

Off you go and cut your traces...

Look for other safer places!

 Wash your hands of the enigmas of Turandot!

(*The Prince has lost all power of resistance. Suddenly,
faint lamentations, not voices, but shadows of voices float
through the darkness of the ramparts. Almost impercepti-
bly, here and there, appear livid and phosphorescent visions.
They are Turandot's lovers, who laid down their lives, un-
able to solve the fatal riddles*)

The voices out of the darkness

Tarry no longer! For if you call her once more we'll see her
for whom we perished! Oh! let us see her!

I love her! I love her! I love her!

(*The visions fade away*)

The unknown Prince (*with a cry*)

No! No! 'Tis I who love her!

The Ministers (*surrounding him*)

Love her? What nonsense! Whom?

Turandot? Ah! Ah! Ah!

 Foolish youth, you're demented!

 Turandot is a phantom and non-existent!

 Like you and all other idiots! and so am I!

 So's everyone, God or mortal!

 You are rushing to destruction like all the other
idiots!

Pu-Tin-Pao! Thou alone art existent! Nought exists but Tao!

The unknown Prince (*still more perplexed*)

But I shall succeed! I'll win her love!

The Ministers

Madman! See what awaits you!

(*They point their index fingers to the summit of the ramparts, where the gigantic form of the executioner appears. He plants the severed head of the young Prince of Persia on a spike*)

The Ministers

'Tis thus the moon will kiss our pallid visage!

(*Timur, in wild desperation clings to his son saying:*)

Timur

My son! Can you bear to abandon me here and to leave your old father to drag out a lonely existance?
Can no one prevail on your heart to have done with this mad undertaking?

Liù (*approaching the Prince and tearfully beseeching him*)

Oh! I entreat thee, Sire, o Sire, to hear me!
Liù can bear no more!
Her weary heart will break, worn with her wandering; thy name alone to sustain her, thy name alone to revive her!
But if on the morrow thy fate should be decided, we must die on the contryside in exile!
He will have lost his only son...
I lost the smile I lived for!...
Liù can bear no more! Hear her cry!

(*She falls to the ground, sobbing and spent*)

The unknown Prince (*approaching her, much moved*)

Oh! weep no more, Liù!
Thou say'st, once long ago,

I smiled upon thee, then for that smile, thou, bravehearted
maiden must heed me:
Thy noble master, perhaps to-morrow, will be left unprotec-
ted...
Thou must not leave him, take him away with thee!
Stay beside him and smooth the path of his exile!
Hear me, hear me, o my poor little Liù
Thy heart cannot refuse him who implores thee,
Cannot refuse him who ne'er will smile again...

*(The ministers, who had drawn aside, once more approach
the Prince, begging and insisting)*

The Ministers

Hear the cry of your father!
Has life no more attractions?

Liù (*in supplication*)

Have pity on us! Hearken to Liù and come!

Timur

For love of me; oh, come!

The Ministers

Why will you be so rash?

The unknown Prince

'Tis I who am asking for pity!
I'll listen no longer!
Her exquisite face is before me!
I see her! She is calling! She is there!

The Ministers (*to Timur*)

Here, get him away, the idiot!
Catch hold of that gibbering maniac!

Timur (*clinging to the Prince*)

Must I be abandoned by thee? My son!
Upon my knees I ask, implore thee! Soften thy heart!

The unknown Prince

O father, pardon thy unhappy son, who'll never smile
again!

Liù

Oh, hear us, I beg, I pray! Oh! hearken, Sire, to me!

The Ministers

He's raving mad! does life not attract you?

Timur

Must I die through thy folly?

The Ministers (*helping to the old man and trying with all
their might to drag Prince away*)

Now, all pull together and get him away!

The unknown Prince

Oh! let me be! You cannot restrain me!
For glory awaits me! I follow my star!

(*A light is thrown on the gong*)

And no mortal arm can restrain me!
When destin calls I follow!

Timur

So long had I lost you and mourned you and now have
I found you and am I to lose you again? For no one has
ever succeeded and each one has paid for his love with
his life!

The Ministers

The face that you see is a phantom!
You're losing your life for a phantom!
For death and perdition await you!
Before you is looming the sword and the scaffold!

Liù

I implore! Oh! hearken, Sir!
For if you should fail and be sent to the scaffold,
We all three together shall die!

Mysterious voices in the distance

> The grave is yawning deep for thee!
> Who darest to challenge love!
> And shades of everlasting gloom
> Will cover your cruel fate!

Liù

> Do not tarry longer!

Timur

> I lie at thy feet! Thou wilt kill thy old father!

Timur-Liù

> 'Tis death!

The Ministers

> 'Tis death.

The unknown Prince (*turning to the Palace, in ecstasy, as if making a supreme offer, he cries:*)

> My passion consumes me and knows no denying!
> All my being is suffering torture!
> Every nerve of my soul and my body is crying:
>
> (*He flings himself against the gong, takes the hammer and strikes thrice ferociously, invoking:*)
>
> Turandot! Turandot! Turandot!
>
> (*Liù and Timur cling to each other in despair. The ministers raise their arms in horror, and rush away exclaiming:*)

The Ministers

> We can hold him no more!
> Our protests are in vain!
> In Sanscrit, in Chinese and every lingo!
> Now he's sounded the gong, death won't be long!
>
> (*The Prince remains in ecstasy at the foot of the gong*)

END OF FIRST ACT

Act second

SCENE I

A pavilion formed by a huge curtain curiously decorated with fantastic and symbolic Chinese figures. The scene is laid on the first floor and has three entrances, one in the centre and two at the sides.

Ping peeps through the middle opening — looks right and left and calls his companions. They enter, followed by three servants, one of whom carries a red lantern, one a green and one a yellow. These they deposit symmetrically in the middle of the stage on a low table surrounded by three stools. The servants then withdraw to the back where they remain squatting.

Ping

Hallo, Pang! Hallo Pong

(mysteriously)

And now the fateful gong has wakened the palace and roused the sleeping city, whatever happens .we are ready: if the stranger is victorious, for the wedding, and, if he loses, ready for the funeral.

Pong *(gaily)*

I'll prepare for the wedding!

Pang *(mournfully)*

And I for the funeral!

Pong

The gay, coloured lanterns of pleasure!

Pang

The gloomy white lanterns of mourning!

Pong

The incense and offerings...

Pang

The incense and offerings...

Pong

And plenty of gilt paper money...

Pang

A lot of tea, sugar and honey!

Pong

A huge scarlet palanquin to ride in!

Pang

A huge gloomy coffin to bide in!

Pong

And bonzes for singing...

Pang

And bonzes for mourning...

Pong-Pang

And everything required according to tradition
Every sort of thing and condition!

Ping (*raising his arms on high*)

O China, O China!
How art thou troubled and shaken in anguish,
That wert so happy, dreaming,
Strong and serene through seventy thousand centuries!

The three

Like a stream everflowing,
Life went on, as it always had been going!
And then came Turandot...

Ping

And now for ages all our jubilations
Are reduced to the following equations:

The three

Three loud bangs on the gong.
  Then three enigmas...
    And a head off!

(*They all three sit down next to the little table on which the servants have laid scrolls, and, as they enumerate, they search through the scrolls*)

Pang

The year of the Mouse, there were six!

Pong

The year of the Dog, there were eight!

Pang

And in the present year, this terrible year ot the Tiger...

The three (*counting on their fingers*)

We have got... to.. number twenty!
That's counting in the stranger!

Ping

How exhausting!

Pong

What a worry!

Ping

What a business!

The three

See to what we three have come!
We're officials of the knife!

(*They drop their scrolls and fall into a comical attitude of wretchedness*)

Ping (*His face clears up and he gazes into the distance with a home-sick expression*)

I've a cottage in Kansou,
Standing on a lake of blue,
All surrounded by bamboo
And I'm here and wasting all my precious life
Racking all my precious brains
          On sacred writings...
Oh! that I were back there too...
By my little lake of blue,
All surrounded by bamboo!...

Pong

I have forests, near Chang-Te.
Finer ones you ne'er could see,
But their shade is not for me,

Pang

I've a garden close to Kiù,
And I left it for this!
Oh shall I ever see you, pretty garden, anymore?

Ping

But I'm here, ever racking my brains on sacred writings!

Pong

Oh! that I were back at Chang...

Pang

Oh! that I were back at Kiù...

Pong

To enjoy my lake of blue,
All surrounded by bamboo!
(*They rise and, with a sweeping gesture of despair, exclaim:*)
O China! O China!
Full of insane and crazy lovers.

Ping

How many hopeful fools we've seen arriving!

Pang

Alas! how many!

Pong

How many!

Pang

How many!

Ping

Do you remember the Imperial Prince of Samarkand?
Scarce had he come a-wooing when she sent for the executioner!

Voices from the inside

Grind and sharpen! till the blade is brightly shining.
Grind and sharpen! till the blade with blood is dripping.

Pong

And the gem-covered Indian, Sagarika,
Who wore such curious bell-shaped earrings?
He asked for love and they cut his head off!

Pang

And the Burmese

Pong

The Prince of Kirghisi?

The three

Beheaded! Beheaded!

Voices from the inside

Grind and sharpen! till the blade with blood is dripping!
In the realm of Turandot, we are newer idle!

Ping

The Tartar, with the bow of seven cubit, arrayed in furry
garments?

The three

> Beheaded! Beheaded!
> All is massacre;... And slaughter!... Unending!...
> Farewell to love and happy laughter!
> Farewell divine race hereafter
> All is over in China!
> (*They return to their seats, with the exception of Ping, who remains standing, to give more emphasis to his invocation*)

Ping (*with his hands raised on high*)

> O Tiger! Tiger! O thou almighty king of the heavens!
> Do thou hasten on that night, which we sigh for!
> The great night of surrender!
> The wedding chamber I shall be preparing!

Pong (*with a descriptive gesture*)

> I shall prepare their couch of downy feathers!

Pang (*as though sprinkling perfumes*)

> In their room I'll scatter sweetest perfumes!

Ping

> The bridal pair I'll guide and bear the lantern!

The three

> And then all three, in the garden, songs of love we will sing until the morning... likes this:
> (*Ping is standing on his stool, the other are seated at his feet and leaning toward an imaginary balcony*)
> Happy is China her Princess no longer hardens her heart and love despises!
> Haughty and cold, she refused to surrender, conquered by love her heart is aglow!
> Noble Princess, thy rule extends from the Tse-Kiang to the mighty Jang-Tse!
> But there, ardent within thy bower, waiteth a spouse who will rule over thee!

In his arms wilt thou learn love's lesson and surrender
thy heart to love!
Glory hail to the night we have prayed for, the mysterious
night that grants our desire!
To the yellow brocaded curtains — to the hour of caresses
and sighs!
Golden night of happy surrender, happy love that unfolds
like a flower...
Night of fragrance and whispering tender, happy hearts,
happy night, happy hour!
Glory, joy to the beautiful maiden, learning the secret of
love evermore!
Glory to him whose devotion shall triumph and to China,
her peace shall restore.

(But, from within, the growing clamour in the palace, recalls the three ministers to the sad reality. Ping, jumping down from his stool, exclaims:)

Ping

But we're dreaming, while the Palace is ablaze with lights
and swarming with servants and soldiers!
You hear them beat the drum of the big green Temple?
The clatter of the clogs upon the Peking pavements!

Pong *(makes a sign to the servants, who remove the lanterns)*

You hear the trumpets? Peace where art thou?

Pang

The trial is beginning!

Ping

Let's go and enjoy the umpteenth torture!

(They go off comically)

END OF SCENE

SCENE II

*The big square in front of the Palace. In the centre is an
enormous marble staircase which ends at the top, under a
triple arch. The staircase has three big landings. Nume-
rous servants place vari-coloured lanterns everywhere. Mandarins are arriving, dressed in ceremonial garments of blue
and gold. The eigth Wise Men pass, tall and pompous.
They are old and very much alike, gaunt and massive of
frame. They move slowly and simultaneously. Each of them
has in his hands three sealed silken scrolls, which contain
the answers to Turandot's enigmas.*

The crowd (*discussing the arrival of the various dignitaries*)

See the eight Wise men arriving,
Full of dignity and learning;
In their scrolls they have the answers
To the ominous enigmas.

*(Incense begins to rise from the tripods at the top of the
staircase.*

*The three Ministers appear through the incense; they are
now dressed in ceremonial coats of yellow).*

The crowd

Here is Ping! Here is Pong! Here is Pang!

*(The white and yellow standards of the Emperor pass
through the clouds of incense, followed by the standards of
war.*

*Gradually the incense disperses and, at the head of the
staircase, seated on a big ivory throne, is seen the Emperor Altoum.*

*He is very old, quite white, venerable, sacred, like a god
appearing through the clouds. The whole crowd falls pro-
state in an attitude of deep respect. The square is bathed
in a rosy light. The Prince stands at the foot of the staircase. Timur and Liù are on the left among the crowd)*

The crowd

> May you live for ever, our Emperor of China!
> Glory be thine!

The Emperor (*with the weary voice of a very old man*)

> A fearful oath has pledged me to this compact, and I
> am bound to it in honour!... Until, alas, my holy sceptre
> reeks of the blood shed! Too much blood shed! Youth,
> get thee hence!

The unknown Prince (*firmly*)

> Son of Heaven! I claim the right to try my fortune!

The Emperor (*almost beseeching him*)

> Will you not let me die without the agonized remorse for
> another young victim?

The unknown Prince (*still more insistently*)

> Son of Heaven! I claim the right to try my fortune!

The Emperor

> Not again, not again will I allow my rule stained by this
> horror!

The unknown Prince (*with increased strength*)

> Son of Heaven! I claim the right to try my fortune!

The Emperor (*with anger but majesty*)

> O madman, rushing to death! So be it!
> Unto thy fate I leave thee!

The crowd (*rising from its knees*)

> Hundred thousand more year to our illustrious Emperor!
> (*A gay procession of women — Turandot's attendants —
> take their places in line on the staircase, scattering flowers.
> When silence is restored, the Mandarin steps forth with
> the decree:*)

The Mandarin

> People of Peking!

The law is this: — Turandot, the Chaste, shall be the bride of him of royal lineage, who shall solve her three enigmas! But he whose attempts are unsuccessful, pays for his failure and shall be beheaded!

Children's voices from the distance

From afar do you hear
A thousand voices sighing clear:
Come, o Princess, down to me!
Summer here will be!

(The Mandarin has hardly withdrawn, when Turandot advances towards the foot of the throne. Beautiful, impassive as a golden image, she glances coldly at the Unknown Prince, who, dazzled at first, gradually recovers his composure and looks at her resolutely. Timur and Liù cannot take their eyes from the Prince. After a solemn silence, Turandot says:)

Turandot

Within this Palace, a thousand thousand years ago, a cry of tortured anguish rent the air; cry of anguish that, travelling down the ages, in my heart has at last found a resting-place! Noble Princess Lo-u-ling, thou example of wisdom, who did'st rule in strict seclusion and glory o'er thy people, and defying with firm, unyielding will the rule of man, thou livest still in me!

The crowd *(very softly)*

'Twas when the King of Tartary displayed his seven red and hostile flags!

Turandot *(evoking distant memories)*

Yet, in those days, as everyone remembers, war broke out with the clash of arms and terror! Her realm was conquered! And Lo-u-ling noble Princess, roughly captured by a man like thee, o stranger, — cruelly dragged to torture, till her imploring voice was still for ever!

The crowd (*murmuring in fervour*)

For ages without number,
Peacefully doth she slumber!

Turandot

Ye Princes, who, in caravans and splendour, from the
four corners of the world come hither, intent to try your
fortune, I will avenge on you — who broke that lily —
that agonizing cry! — Ne'er shall I be wed! Ne'er shall man
posses me! The hate of him who killed her lives in my
heart for e'er! No! Never mortal man! Ah! I ne'er will
betray the glory of such chastity!

(*menacingly to the Prince*)

Then, stranger! Do not challenge thy fortune!
My enigmas none can solve, so death must follow!

The unknown Prince

No! No! The enigmas I shall solve and life will follow!

The crowd

Now must the valiant stranger be allowed the trial, o Turandot!

(*The trumpets sound. Silence. Turandot proclaim the first
enigma*)

Turandot

Then listen, o stranger! « In the night's dark shadow,
bright and elusive, hovers a phantom. Upward it soars
and spreads its wings above the gloomy human crowd. Everybody invokes it and everybody implores it. But the
phantom, which vanishes at dawn, is born again in every
heart! And every night 'tis born and every day it
dies! »

(*A short silence*)

The unknown Prince (*with sudden impulse*)

Yes! Born again! 'Tis born again exulting and carries me away, Turandot: for 'tis « Hope ».

The wise men (*rise and automatically unroll the first scroll together*)

'Tis Hope! 'Tis Hope! 'Tis Hope!

(*Then, together they seat themselves again. In the crowd is heard a murmur of surprise, which is immediately checked by a sign from a dignitary*)

Turandot (*looks around her proudly — smiles coldly — regains her composure and says:*)

Yes! it is hope that falsely lures you onward!

(*She comes nervously halfway down the staircase, as if to fascinate and confuse the Prince and propounds the second enigma:*)

« Like a flame it is flaring, yet it is no flame! Sometimes it is delirium! and fever, burning and ardent! Inertia will transmute it into languor! If your life you are losing, it grows cold! But when you dream of conquest, it is flaming! When you hearken to its voice you are a-tremble! and, like the sunset, 'tis dyed in crimson glow »!

(*The Prince hesitates. Turandot's gaze seems to confuse him. He seeks whitin his mind, but does not find the answer. The Princess has an expression of triumph in her eyes*)

The Emperor

Think well and long, o stranger!

The crowd

Your life's at stake! Answer!

Liù (*beseechingly*)

It is for love's sake!

The unknown Prince (*Suddenly losing his look of despair, he hurls these words at Turandot*)

Yes mighty Princess! It flames and yet doth languish —
Yes, when thine eyes in mine are gazing: 'tis « Blood ».

The wise men (*opening the second scroll*)

'Tis Blood! 'Tis Blood! 'Tis Blood!

The crowd

Take courage, thou who solvest the enigmas!

Turandot (*pointing to the crowd, shouts to the guards*)

Make these wretches be quiet!

(*She comes to the bottom of the staircase and leans towards the Prince who falls on his knees. With ferocity, accenting every syllable, her lips almost touching his face, she gives him the third enigma*)

« Ice that fire doth give thee and from thy fire more ice is begotten! Clear as day, yet inscrutable! The force that will you free, a slave will make you! Yet, accepting you as slave, will make you King! »...

The unknown Prince (*scarcely breathing, makes no reply. Turandot, bending over him as over a prey, says sneeringly:*)

Turandot

Now surrender! Your cheeks are white with terror!
For you know it is hopeless! Tell me, stranger!
The ice that turns to fire, what can it be?

The unknown Prince (*in desolation rests his head in his hands: but for a second only. An expression of joy comes over his countenance, and bounding to his feet, magnificent in his pride and strength, he exclaims:*)

Ah! thou hast told me; my life to thee I owe!
And my fire shall dissolve thee: « Turandot! »
(*Turandot staggers, steps back and remains immovable at the foot of the stairs, petrified with scorn and grief*)

The wise men (*who have unrolled the third scroll, exclaim:*)
Turandot! Turandot! Turandot!

The crowd (*with a shout*)
                    Turandot!
Glory, glory to the conqueror!
Thine is life and triunph, thime is life and love!
Everlasting glory to our illustrious Emperor!
Light and Ruler of all the Universe!

Turandot (*who, at the first cry, has roused herself, filled with anguish, goes up the stair again, close to the Emperor's throne, and pleads:*)
Hear me, my father! Son of Heaven!
Thou can'st not throw thy daughter in the arms of this unknown stranger!

The Emperor (*solemnly*)
My sacred oath is binding!

Turandot (*rebelliously*)
No, thou can'st not! Thy daughter is sacred!
Thou can'st not give me to him, as though I were a slave, almost dead with shame and loathing!
(*angrily to the Prince*)
Do not look thus at me!
Thou who mockest my pride!
I'll not be thine! No, I will not!

The Emperor (*still more solemnly*)
My sacred oath is binding!

The crowd

The sacred oath is binding!

Turandot

No, I'll not surrender!
No man shall win me!

The crowd

The Prince has triumphed, Princess!
He staked his life to win thee!
And he must be rewarded!

Turandot (*turning to the Prince*)

Unwillingly in thine arms woulst have me?
In thine arms? Ah, never!

The unknown Prince

No! No! thou haughty Princess!
I want thee ardent with love!

The crowd

Be undaunted! Show thy courage! Intrepid!

The unknown Prince

You set me three enigmas! All three I solved!
Now only one I will give to thee to solve!
My name is unknown!
Tell me my name before the morning and, at break of day,
I'll die!

(*Turandot accepts his challenge with an affirmative sign.
The Emperor rises and, deeply moved, says:*)

The Emperor

I pray the heavens that, at break of day, thou shalt be
my son!

(*The Court rises. The trumpets sound. Banners are waved.
The Prince, holding his head high, and with a firm step,
mounts the staircase, whilst the Imperial Hymn is played solemnly and sung by all the people*)

The crowd

At thy feet we prostrate fall.
Light and Ruler of the Universe!
For thy wond'rous wisdom and thy piety,
All our hearts are thine,
Full of joy and pride!
All our homage and our love!
Everlasting glory to our illustrious Emperor!
With thee, great scion of Hien-Wang, we rejoice!
Everlasting glory to our illustrious Emperor!
Raise on high the banners!
Glory to thee!

END OF SECOND ACT

Act third

SCENE I

The Palace garden, very vast and undulating; between the bushes are bronze divinities, lightly illuminated from below by the reflex of the glow from the incense-burners.

On the right, five steps lead to a Pavilion, closed by a richly-embroidered curtain. This Pavilion forms an ante-chamber to one of the wings of the Palace on the side of Turandot's chambers. It is Night. From very far are heard the voices of the Heralds proclaiming the Royal edict all over the city. Other voices, from near and far, re-echo the order.

Reclining on the steps of the pavilion, in the silence of the night, the unknown Prince listens to the Heralds, as if he were living in another world.

The voices of the heralds

'Tis thus decreed by Turandot:
« In Peking », she commands « no one shall sleep to-night »

Voices in the distance (*plaintively*)

None shall sleep to-night! None shall sleep to-night!

The voices of the heralds (*further off*)

« On pain of death, the name of the stranger shall be discoved ere break of morning! »...

Voices in the distance

On pain of death! On pain of death!

The voices of the heralds (*still further off*)

« In Peking », she commands « no one shall sleep to-night! »

Voices in the distance

None shall sleep to-night! None shall sleep to-night
(*The re-echoing of voices and the sound of the gong are
lost in the distance*)

The unknown Prince

None shall sleep to-night!... Princess, thou too art waking,
In thy lonely chamber, watching the stars which throb
with love and longing!
Within my heart my secret lies
And what my name is none shall know!
Till on thy heart I confess it,
As soon as morning light shall dawn!
Princess, then shall my kisses break the silence that makes
thee mine!...

Women's voices (*mysterious and rather distant*)

Ah! what his name is none shall know...
And all of us, alas, shall die!...

The unknown Prince

O night depart! O ye stars, grow paler!
At daybreak she'll be mine at last!
(*The three Ministers emerge from the bushes, followed
by a small crowd of figures dim in the darkness of the
night and gradually increasing in number*)

Ping (*approaching the Prince*)

Take your eyes off the stars above and give us your
attention!

Pang

Do you not know, our life is in your power!

Pong

We're in your power!

Ping

You heard the order? Through the valleys and highways throughout the city, death and destruction are crying: « Who is he? »

All three

Who art thou? O tell us!

The unknown Prince (*in the defensive*)

Well, what is it you ask?

Ping

Say what you want! Is it love you are seeking? 'Tis here, then take it!

(*He pushes forward a group of alluringly beautiful and seminude maidens*)

Look! How lovely! Behold their rare, alluring beauty!

Pong-Pang (*extolling their beauty*)

Sinuous bodies!...

Ping

Enrapturing visions of happiness enchanting!

(*The maidens surround the Prince, who, resisting, cries:*)

The unknown Prince

No!... No!...

The three Ministers

Then what?... Possessions?
See, all this wealth is thine!

(*At a sign, baskets, chests and bags filled with gold and precious stones are brought in. The three Ministers dangle these splendours before the dazzled eyes of the Prince*)

Pong

Lighting the darkest shadows...
See these glittering jewels!

Pong

Pearls and diamonds!

Pang

Opal and sapphire!

Pong

Emerald and topaz!

Pang

And rubies gleaming rosy red!

Ping

Golden fragments of star-land!
Take them all! they are thine! All thine!

The unknown Prince (*still resisting*)

No! away with your riches!

The three (*with increasing eagerness*)

Would'st thou have glory?
We will assist thy flight! And far away beyond the mountains,
Thou shalt be the Ruler of the Empire!...

All

Do not tarry! Cruel death awaits you.
Oh! haste away! Save thyself and all of us!...

The unknown Prince (*raising his arms in invocation*)

Hasten, morning! Dispel this awful nightmare!...

(*The three Ministers get closer to him and, in despairs, say:*)

Ping

Oh! stranger, you don't know all the torture and agonizing pain in store for us!

Pong-Pang

All the ghastly new devices of torture that we shall suffer, if you stay here and still refuse to reveal to us your name!

All

> For she is unrelenting! — Alas, we shall all be slaughter'd
> — Oh! what a terrible shambles! — The sharpened knife
> — The wheel of torture — The burning grip of red-hot
> pincer! — A death drawn out by inches! — Oh! save
> us from death!

The unknown Prince (*absolutely firm*)

> In vain are your entreaties!
> In vain your threats and warnings!
> The world may die, but I want Turandot!
>
> (*The crowd loses all controll and roars savagely around
> the Prince*)

All

> You shall not! Before you have her you'll die at our
> hands!
> Accursed scoundrel! Answer us! Your name!
> Tell us who art thou?
>
> (*They hold their daggers menacingly against the Prince,
> who is sore pressed, surrounded by the ferocious and de-
> sperate crowd. Suddenly, loud cries heard proceeding from
> the garden — all stop:*)

The voices

> Here is the name! It is here!
>
> (*A group of city guards are seen dragging Timur and Liù
> ragged, bruised, exhausted, bleeding. The crowd becomes
> silent and is full of anxiety and exspectation. The Prince
> rushes towards them, crying:*)

The unknown Prince

> These two know nothing!... However should they know it?...
>
> (*But Ping recognized the two, and in great exultation,
> cries:*)

Ping

That old man and the maiden were talking with you
yesterday!

The unknown Prince

Let go of them!

Ping

Of course, they know your secret!
(*to the soldiers*)

Were did you come across them?

The soldiers

They were wandering beside the ramparts!

Ping (*running towards the Pavilion*)

Mighty Princess!

All

Royal Princess!
(*Turandot appears — they all fall prostrate on the ground...
Only Ping advances with great humility and says:*)

Ping

Most illustrious Princess!... The name you would discover
is held within the lips of this couple... But we have tools
wherewith to prize them open and we have pincers that will
drag out the name!
(*The Prince, who had controlled himself to avoid self-
betrayal, on hearing the cruel jest and the threat, shows
signs of fierce resentment: but Turandot stops him with an
imperious and ironical look.*)

Turandot

Ah! you are growing paler!

The unknown Prince (*haughtily*)

'Tis but thy terror, seeing the dawn of day upon my visage!
These two do not know who I am!

Turandot

> Thou liest!

(Turning to Timur, she commands resolutely)

I bid you answer!

(She awaits the reply, sure of herself and almost indifferent, but the old man is silent. Dulled by pain, his venerable locks dishevelled, pale, tattered and bloodstained, he looks at the Princess in silence, his eyes veiled and with an expression of supplication)

Turandot

I order you to answer! Who is he?

(Timur is seized again, but before the Prince has time to act and defend him, Liù quickly comes forward and, facing Turandot, cries:)

Liù

The name you want is known to no one but me!

The crowd *(with a cry)*

We are delivered! Saved from certain death!

The unknown Prince *(proudly reprimanding Liù)*

Thou knowest nothing! Nothing!

Liù *(gazing at the Prince with infinite tenderness, turns to Turandot and says:)*

> ...I know his name,

and the height of my joy is to keep his secret locked within my heart!

The crowd *(seeing their hopes vanish, surround Liù crying)*

Clap her into chains and flay her! Make her answer or behead her!

The unknown Prince *(standing in front of Liù to protect her, threateningly)*

You shall pay for all her suffering!
You shall pay for all her torment!

Turandot (*violently to the guards*)

Arrest the man!

Liù (*firmly to the Prince*)

My lord! I shall not speak!

(*A soldier shackles the Prince's feet and holds the rope-ends, while two other soldiers seize hold of his arms. Turandot resumes her aloof attitude, whilst Liù, seized by her torturers, has fallen to the ground in a kneeling position*)

Ping (*bending over her*)

His name!

Liù (*sweetly, imploringly*)

No!...

Ping (*furiously*)

His name!

Liù

I humbly ask for your pardon, but I cannot tell!

(*At a sign from Ping, the soldier twists her wrists — Liù screams. At that moment Timur rouses himself from his terrible silence*)

Timur

What was that scream?

The unknown Prince

Let go of her!...

Liù

No... No... I'll scream, no more! They are not hurting! No, no one has hurt me!

(*to the soldiers*)

Come on then... but gag me, I beg you, lest he should hear me!

(*weakening*)

I can stand no more!

The crowd (*in strangled tones*)
Answer! What's his name?

Turandot
Set her free now!... Answer!
(*Liù is freed*)

Liù
I rather will die!
(*She falls helpless on the steps of the pavilion*)

Turandot
(*Looking at Liù in an effort to penetrate the mystery*)
What can it be that gives thee such endurance?

Liù
Mighty Princess, my love!...

Turandot

Thy love?

Liù (*raising her eyes, full of tenderness*)
Such the love that I bear him, such true devotion, secret
and deep, that all these tortures are but sweetness to me,
because I gladly give them to my loved one...
For, by my silence, I shall give him thy love...
Thine shall he be, Princess, while I lose everything!
Yea, even to the hope that I know is hopeless!
(*turning to the soldiers*)
Renew my fetters if you will!
Imprison me in chains! Torture me!
Ah! I am offering my life, my love's crowning glory!

Turandot (*who, for a moment, felt fascinated and confused
by Liù's words, now gives an order to the Ministers*)
She shall reveal the secret!

Ping

Go send for Pu-Tin-Pao!

The unknown Prince (*struggling violentiy*)

No! You accursed barbarians!

The crowd (*yelling*)

Behead her! Behead her! Behead her!

Ping

She must be racked and tortured!

The crowd (*savagely*)

Let her be tortured! Yes, behead her! Answer!

(*And now the gigantic figure of the executioner Pu-Tin-Pao, with his assistants, appear in the background, rigid and fearful.*

Liù utters a desperate cry, she rushes around like one demented, trying vainly to break through the crowd, imploring and supplicating.)

Liù

I can no longer! I am losing my strength!...
Release me, I implore you! Oh! let me go, I beg you!

The crowd (*barring the ways*)

Answer! Answer!

Liù (*in despair, running to Turandot*)

Yes, I will answer thee, Princess!...
Thou, who with ice art girdled, must melt beneath such passion, and his love shall waken thine! For, ere the day is breaking, his secret within me taking, my eyes shall close for ever... to see his face no more!...
Yes, when the stars are waning, the pale stars are waning, my eyes shall close for ever... to see is face no more!

(*In a flash, she snatches a sharp dagger from the belt of a soldier and stabs herself mortally. She looks at the Prin-*

*ce with intense tenderness, staggers towards him and falls
at his feet — dead)*

The crowd (*yelling*)

Answer! His name!

The unknown Prince

Ah! you have died for me, o my poor little Liù.

(*Deep silence pervades and a feeling of terror.*

*Turandot looks at Liù lying on the ground, then with an
expression of anger seizes a whip from the executioner's
assistant and strikes the soldier who allowed Liù to snatch
his dagger, full in the face. The soldier covers his face
with his hands and disappears in the crowd.*

The Prince is freed

*Timur, almost crazed, staggers to where Liù's body lies,
and, kneeling beside her, says:*)

Timur

Liù... Liù... Come!... Rise!..

It is the hour when day is breakin! 'Tis
morning, little Liù, open your eyes, my darling!

(*An intense feeling of pity, of confusion and remorse pervades. Turandot's face reflects an expression of torment.
Ping notices it and goes over to the old man to order him
away roughly. However, as he approaches him, his cruelty
and harshness give way to a kinder feeling*)

Ping

Come away, old man! She's dead!

Timur (*with a cry*)

Ah! accursed outrage! Poor innocent victim!
Vengeance will surely follow us all from on high!

(*A superstitious fear seizes the crowd. Terror that the dead
girl will become a malignant spirit, because she had been*

*the victim of an injustice, and be transformed, according
to the people's belief, into a vampire.*

*Whilst two maidens cover Turandot's face with a silvery
white veil, the crowd, in supplication says:)*

The crowd

Dolorous spirit, do not punish us!
O martyred spirit, grante us thy pardon!

*(With religious fervour, the little corpse is carried away
by the crowd, who show their deep respect.*

The old man approaches and walks near her, saying:)

Timur

Liù!... So good! Liù'!... so gentle!
Come let us once more take the road together

(Tenderly takes the girl's little hand in his)

Like this — thy little hand in mine to guide me!
I shall follow thee. I know where thou art gone and I
shall rest beside thee in the night which has no morning!

*(The three old Ministers are greatly distressed, as they feel
awakening in their souls their old human compassion)*

Ping

Never can I remember to have looked upon death without
a snigger!

Pang *(striking his chest)*

Tenderness, long forgotten, awakes and stirs my heart
with woe and pity!

Pong

Poor little martyred maiden, thou wilt weigh on my heart
and soul for ever!

(The sad procession moves away and the crowd departs)

The crowd

> Liù forgive us, grant us thy pardon!
> Liù so good! Liù so gentle! Forget! O lovely spirit!
>
> *(The voices are lost in the distance. All have gone.
> The Prince and Turandot remain alone, facing each other.
> The Princess rigid and statuesque under ample veil, motionless)*

The unknown Prince *(with intense and vibrant force)*

> Thou with heart unrelenting
> Cold as ice, unrelenting!
> Come then forth from thy portals,
> Down to earth with us mortals!...
> Tear thy veil asunder!...
> Look in pity and wonder,
> On this innocent maiden,
> Whom you sent to her death!
>
> *(He rushes towards her and tears off her veil)*

Turandot *(authoritatively)*

> Ah! unhand me! How dare you?
> I am no human being...
> But the daughter of heaven...
> Your daring hand may tear my veil asunder, my soul is
> far, far away!

The unknown Prince *(who, for a moment, remains spellbound, draws back. He regains his composure and, with ardent audacity retorts:)*

> Yes, thy soul may be yonder, but thy body is beside me!
> And, with rapturous fingers, I'm caressing the gold-embroidered hem of thy mantle!
> While my passionate kisses I imprint on thy lips!...
>
> *(He approaches Turandot with outstretched arms)*

Turandot *(drawing back in confusion, frightened, desperate, but threatening)*

> Do not profane me!...

The unknown Prince (*desperately*)
Ah! to feel thee living!

Turandot
Unhand me!

The unknown Prince
Thy heart is ice no longer and mine thou art!

Turandot
No... No one shall win me!
My ancestor's cries still are ringing in my ears!
Ah! No!

The unknown Prince
You're mine I say.

Turandot
Dare not to touch me, stranger! 'Twere sacrilegious!

The unknown Prince
No! a kiss from thee begets eternal life!
(*In saying these words strong in the convinction of his right and of his love, he takes Turandot in his arms and kisses her passionately. Turandot offers no resistance against so much impetuosity, her voice fails her, she has no more strength or will. The bewildering contact has transfigured her. With accents of supplication, almost childlike, she murmurs:*)

Turandot
What hast thou done?... Have pity!...

The unknown Prince
My flower! Oh, my rare unfolding flower;
Thy fragrance I am breathing!
Thy bosom, white as marble, upon my breast is trembling!
In my arms, I can feel thee, faint with sweetness!
Fair as lily in thy silvery mantle!

Turandot (*her eyes veiled with tears*)
  Thou hast conquered!

The unknown Prince (*in ecstatic tenderness*)
  Weepest thou?

Turandot (*shivering*)
                'Tis morning!
  (*in a whisper*)
  Turandot is vanquished!

The unknown Prince (*with intense passion*)
  'Tis morning... And love wakes with the sunshine!
  (*Out of the silence of the garden where the last shades of night are fading, soft fresh voices arise and soar like sounds ethereal*)

The voices
  Morning!... Light and glory!
  All is radiant! All is holy!
  Happy Princess! Sweetness mingles in thy weeping!

Turandot
  Ah! let no one see me...
  (*with sweet resignation*)
  For my glory is over!

The unknown Prince
  No! Now 'tis beginning!

Turandot
                Shamed am I!

The unknown Prince
  Oh! miracle! For thy glory arises from the magic of thy first caresses, thy first tears flowing!

Turandot (*transformed, exaltedly*)

My first tears flowing!... Ah!...
I never wept before! But, when I saw thee, o'er my
quivering senses stole a grim foreboding of this disastrous
ending.
Ah! how many have I seen die for me!
And have despised them, but was afraid of thee!...
For from thine eye was shining the assurance of success!
Yes, for thine eye was shining with the radiance of victory...
And for that did I hate thee...
And for that did I love thee,
Torn hither and thither by two conflicting terrors:
Conquer thee or be conquered... And conquered I am!...
Not so much by the solved enigmas, as by this fever which
I get from thee!

The unknown Prince

I've won thee!... Won thee!

Turandot

This, then, which thou art seeking, thou hast achieved!
Depart, for thou art victorious! Depart, o stranger, with
thy name unknown!

The unknown Prince (*impetuously*)

My name unknown? — Nay, unknown no longer!
You, who swoon beneath my kisses!
You who tremble at my ardour,
Can kill me, if you will, for my name, with my life,
I freely give you?
I am Calaf, son of Timur!

Turandot (*at this unforeseen and unexpected revelation,
suddenly feels her pride rekindled and replies ferociously*)

I know thy name!... Ah! I know it.

Calaf

I have no glory but thy kiss!

Turandot

Hearken! Trumpets are sounding.

Calaf

I have no life but in thine arms!

Turandot

Hearken! 'tis morning!

'Tis the hour of trial!

Calaf

I do not fear it!

Turandot (*drawing herself up, regally, majestically*)

Come Calaf, before the people with me!

Calaf

Now thou hast won!
(*They walk towards the rear.
The trumpets sound louder. The heavens radiate light*)

THE SCENE DISSOLVES

SCENE II

The outside of the Imperial Palace, all sculptured in white marble, tinted like flowers by the rosy reflection of the dawn.

On a high staircase in the centre of the scene, is the Emperor, surrounded by his court, his dignitaries, wise men and soldiers.

On both sides of the square the huge crowd forms a wide semi-circle.

The crowd

Hundred thousand more years to our illustrious Emperor!

(The three Ministers spread a mantle of cloth of gold on the ground, as Turandot walks up the staircase.

Suddenly there is silence.

And in the silence of that moment, the Princess exclaims:)

Turandot

Royal father, 'tis dawn... I know the name of the stranger!

(Then looking straight at Calaf, who is at the foot of the staircase, vanquished, she murmurs sweetly, almost with a sigh:)

And his name is... love!

(Calaf rushes up the staircase and the lovers embrace, whilst the crowd, with outstretched hands, scatters flowers and shouts for joy:)

The crowd

O love for all eternity!
Love is the torch that burns for ever,
And in love we exult,
In gratitude for safety and happiness!
                    Glory, evermore!

END OF OPERA